The Early Reader's

Big Book
of Bible
Learning

THE EARLY READER'S BIG BOOK OF BIBLE LEARNING

published by Gold'n'Honey Books
a part of the Questar publishing family

© 1995 by V. Gilbert Beers
Illustrations © 1995 by Terri Steiger

International Standard Book Number: 0-88070-774-7

Printed in the United States of America

For information:
QUESTAR PUBLISHERS, INC.
POST OFFICE BOX 1720
SISTERS, OREGON 97759

95   96   97   98   99   00   01   02 — 10   9   8   7   6   5   4   3   2   1

The Early Reader's

Big Book
of Bible
Learning

BY V. Gilbert Beers

ILLUSTRATIONS BY Terri Steiger

Gold 'n'
Honey
BOOKS

Jeremy's House Has Only One Room

Hi. Welcome to our village.

My name is Jeremy. I live in this house.

Most people in our little village have houses like this.

Would you like to come in and visit me?

During the day we are outside most of the time.

No one stays inside our house much

when the sun is shining.

This is our yard. It has a wall around it.

The wall is made of mud bricks.

Our yard is small, as you can see.

But we cook out here most of the time.

Do you see that hole in the middle?

That is our stove where my mother cooks.

She burns sticks or thorns for the fire.

Sometimes she finds dried grass.

I wish we had charcoal, like people in the city.

How do we start the fire?

We hit a stone on some flint.

The sparks start a fire.

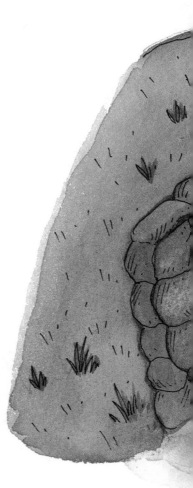

Do you see our donkey?

Do you see our goats?

Do you see our chickens?

They all live here with us.

Our donkey carries things for us.

My father rides him too.

If he doesn't, he must walk.

Look at the walls of our house.

They are bricks.

They are made of dry mud.

Mud holds them together.

Be careful! A snake sometimes hides in the cracks.

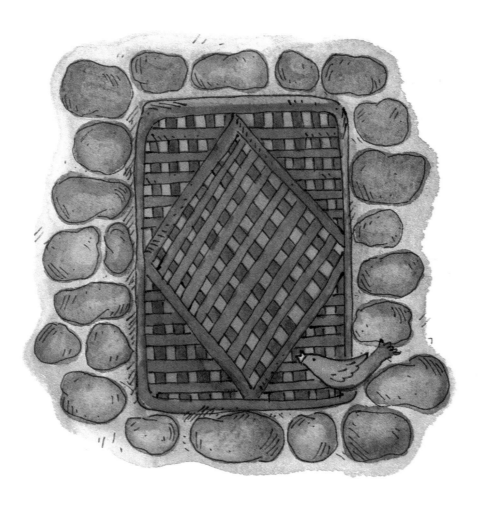

Do you see the window?

It is only a hole in the wall.

My father put strips of wood over it.

Now people and animals can't get through it.

Our door is made of sycamore wood.

If we had more money, we could use cedar wood.

We open our door when the sun comes up.

We close it when the sun goes down.

People who are traveling can stop here to eat.

When the door is closed, we will not let them in.

We are afraid of robbers at night.

Our house keeps us safe.

The door is open. Let's go inside.

We sit on mats during the day.

At night we sleep on them.

Some neighbors have a chair or stool to sit on.

Do you see the hole in the floor?

Do you see the fire in it? That is our stove.

When it is cold or raining, we cook over it.

The fire keeps us warm.

The smoke goes up.

We hope it goes out the window at the top of the wall.

Do you see the chest over there?

We keep most of our things in it.

We have only one room.

It is our bedroom.

It is our living room.

It is our kitchen.

It is our dining room.

We do not have a bathroom. We go outside.

When we wash, we use that big clay pitcher and bowl.

At night, we sleep in a row on our mats.

My father sleeps at one end.

My mother sleeps at the other end.

My brother and sisters and I sleep between them.

That helps us keep warm.

Would you like to see our roof?

Up here on the roof, you can see other houses all around.

In the summer we eat up here and sleep up here.

We sit and talk up here.

The little wall around the roof keeps us from falling off.

We store many things up here.

Do you see the stalks of flax?

My mother will make clothing from the flax.

Do you see the big jars?

They are filled with grain.

It is drying up here.

That fruit in the clay bowl is drying up here too.

Thank you for coming to my house.

I like it here.

I thank God for my house every day.

Do you?

Why Can't I Turn on the Faucet?

In Bible times there were no faucets.

There were no bathtubs like ours.

There were no kitchen sinks like ours.

Bible-time people had to go to a well or

cistern to get water.

The women carried the water from the well.

This is how they carried it.

The big pot on the woman's head is

made of clay.

Can you carry a pot like that?

At the well a woman let the big jar down with a rope.

The jar went down into the water.

When it was full, the woman pulled it up.

Then she put the jar on her head.

She carried the jar home.

The wells were not very wide.

But they went down farther than a big tree goes up.

How did they get so deep?

Men had to dig them.

How would you like to dig a well?

It was hard work.

It's easy to get water today.

Have you thanked God today for water?

Let's Lie Down and Eat Our Lunch

Where do you eat your lunch?

Most of the time you sit on a chair.

You put your lunch on a table.

Sometimes you eat your lunch with a

fork, a spoon, and a knife.

In Jesus' time, many people lay down to

eat their lunch or dinner. They called this reclining.

One night, Jesus and His friends went to a home in Jerusalem.

They went to a room upstairs.

They reclined to eat in that room.

This was the last meal Jesus had with them before He died.

How did people eat this way?

They leaned back on cushions.

The left arm held them up.

Then they stretched out their feet.

How would you like to eat this way?

That Bread Looks Like Pizza

That is Bible-time bread.

It looks like pizza without all the pizza goodies on top.

Bible-time bread is much like the bread part of our pizza

today. It's thin. It's round.

Sometimes people punched holes in it.

It doesn't look much like a loaf of bread at your grocery store.

It doesn't even taste much like bread today.

It's chewy, like pizza bread.

That's the way Bible-time people made bread.

Thank You, Lord, for bread to eat.

I'll take it either way.

Are Those Things Really Bottles?

Those things don't look much like our bottles, do they?

They are not glass.

They are not even plastic.

What are they?

Bible-time people did not know how to make plastic.

They didn't know how to make glass bottles either.

So they made their bottles with animal skins.

Sometimes the skins got old and cracked.

Then they had to be thrown away.

What things do you keep inside bottles at your house?

What kinds of things do you see inside

bottles at the grocery store?

Bible-time people did not have most of these things.

They had wine and milk.

That was about all they could put in the skin bottles.

What could you not have with Bible-time bottles only?

How would grocery shopping be different?

Are you glad for bottles today?

Would you rather have these big animal skin bottles?

Will You Please Turn On the Light?

You flip a switch. The electric lights go on.

They light the room. They light your house.

You even have lights outside your house.

You could not flip a switch in Bible times.

They did not have electricity.

So they did not have electric lights.

When the sun went down people closed their doors.

Their houses were dark.

So people lit lamps like this.

Most homes had only one lamp.

The lamp was made of clay.

The clay was hard now.

People squeezed oil from olives.

They poured this olive oil into the lamp.

They poured it through the big hole in the top.

A wick was put in the small hole of the lamp.

It went down into the olive oil.

The wick was made of flax.

People put the lamp on a stand.

Or they put it on a ledge in a wall.

The lamp burned all night.

That was the only light a Bible-time home had.

The Bible-time lamp gave about the

same light as a candle today.

A child cries. Something makes a noise.

The Bible-time person was glad for the lamp.

Are you glad for all the lights in your home?

Thank You, Lord!

Time to Clean Up

In Bible times, only some rich people had bathtubs.

But they did not have faucets.

They could not get hot and cold water the way we get it.

Most people had to go to a well to get their water.

Most people would get clean like this.

They would pour water in a big basin.

They would take what we call a sponge bath.

They would not have enough water to get in it.

Instead, they would wash themselves the way

you would wash your hands.

To have warm water, they would put water in a water pot.

They let it sit in the sun during the day.

Then they would pour it in the basin.

Other people had streams or rivers nearby.

It was easy to take a bath there.

Taking a bath had one more step.

Many people put olive oil on their bodies after a bath.

Rich people had olive oil with perfume in it.

Poor people did not have money for this.

So they used olive oil without the perfume.

This is how the olive tree looked.

Do you see the olives?

The oil squeezed from the olives was

kept in little jars like these.

Could I Buy Jeans at the Clothing Store?

You couldn't buy a pair of jeans in Bible times.

They didn't have them. And they did not have clothing stores.

In Bible times, your mother would probably make

all your clothing. This took many, many hours.

So people did not have much clothing.

Usually they wore the same clothes every day.

They even wore them at night.

That's because they had no pajamas or

other special night clothing.

Girls and boys wore almost the

same kinds of clothing.

Girls' clothing was more fancy.

Their clothes did not have buttons or zippers.

Most of their clothing did not have collars or sleeves.

Sandals were much like our sandals today.

They were wood or leather.

A tunic was like a nightshirt.

Bible-time people did not have underclothes like ours.

Girls and boys wore a tunic next to their body.

That was their underclothes.

The cloak or coat was like a bathrobe today.

Girls and boys wore this over the tunic.

They wore a wide belt around the waist.

When a person ran, he tucked this tunic and

cloak into the belt. This was called girding.

Girls wore scarves on their heads.

The scarf could be wrapped over their face.

This became a veil to hide their face.

Boys wore a turban.

It was like a big scarf.

It kept the sun and wind

from the boy's neck and head.

Clothes took many hours to make.

First, people had to grow the flax, or cotton.

Or they had to raise sheep, and shear the sheep

to get the wool.

A mother and daughter would spin

the wool or flax or cotton into thread.

Then they wove the threads into cloth.

They used a loom to do this.

Then they had to cut and sew the cloth to make clothes.

You can see why it took so long.

When clothes tore, people did not throw them away.

They mended them. Clothes were passed from father to son.

They were passed from mother to daughter.

Think about this when you go in a clothing store.

It's so easy today to buy clothing.

Have you thanked God today for what you wear?

A Visit to Abraham's Tent

Would you like to come to my home? This is it!

My name is Isaac.

I live in this tent with my father Abraham and

my mother Sarah.

What does my father do for a living?

He has sheep, goats, and cattle. He has camels, too.

Our animals eat grass here.

They drink water in a stream nearby.

But when they have eaten most of the grass, we move.

We take our tent down.

We go away to another place with more grass and water.

Where did we get this tent?

Our servants made it.

They made it from goats' hair.

If we had been poor, my mother would have made it.

Do you see how we put up the tent?

We put poles up first.

Then we tie the tent to the poles with ropes.

The ropes are made of goats' hair, too.

My mother has her own tent.

If we were poor, she would have another room in this tent.

The girls in the family would stay with her.

Where is our kitchen? We do not have one.

Do you see the hole outside the tent?

It has stones around it.

We cook over a fire in this hole.

Where is our bedroom?

We do not have that either.

We put straw mats on the floor.

We sleep on the mats.

We spread an animal skin on the dirt floor.

That is our table.

Do you see my sister churning butter?

The churn is an animal skin sewed together.

My sister will shake the milk until the butter forms.

Do you see the clay pots? Those are our dishes.

A servant woman is grinding flour at the mill.

If we were poor, my mother would do that.

The animal skin hanging from a branch is a bottle of water.

We do not have glass bottles like yours.

Are you glad for your home?

Can you thank God now for the helpful and

beautiful things in your home?

The Most Wonderful House in the World

The world's most wonderful house wasn't really a

house like yours. It was God's house.

But it wasn't a church like yours.

It was called a temple. King Solomon had

this temple built. His father was King David.

David gave the money to build the temple.

He gave about 36 billion dollars in gold.

He also gave silver, wood and stone.

And that was just the beginning. That is much, much more

than our buildings cost today. There are probably a few huge

buildings today that cost a billion dollars. But not many.

There were 180,000 workers who built the temple.

It took them seven years to build it.

The temple became a 40 billion dollar house.

No other building has ever cost so much.

This is the way it looked outside. Let's look closer.

Around the temple were many walls and pillars.

There were many big open spaces called courtyards.

In front of the temple was a big altar.

Priests burned meat on this altar.

That was an offering to God.

There was also a huge wash basin.

It was called the laver.

Priests had to wash their hands and feet here before

they went inside.

This is how the laver and altar looked.

There were only two rooms inside the temple.

Only priests could go into them.

Each day a priest would go into

the first room.

It was called the Holy Place.

He burned incense on a golden altar.

He took care of the golden table with bread on it.

That was called the table of showbread.

He kept the seven golden oil lamps burning.

The other room was called the Holy of Holies.

Only once a year did a priest go inside it.

A beautiful golden chest was there.

It had angel-like figures on it.

The stone tablets with the

Ten Commandments were in this chest.

This chest was called the Ark of the Covenant.

Why Are You Pouring Oil on My Head?

Someone pours oil on your head.

Would you be angry? Or would you be glad?

This happened often in Bible times.

It was called being anointed.

Kings were often anointed.

So were priests and high priests.

So were some prophets.

Often a high priest would anoint someone because

God told him to. Samuel anointed David.

This showed that David would become king.

This is how Samuel did it.

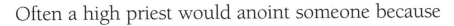

The oil was olive oil.

It was squeezed from olives.

Sometimes perfume was added to it.

The oil was poured from an animal horn.

It looked like this.

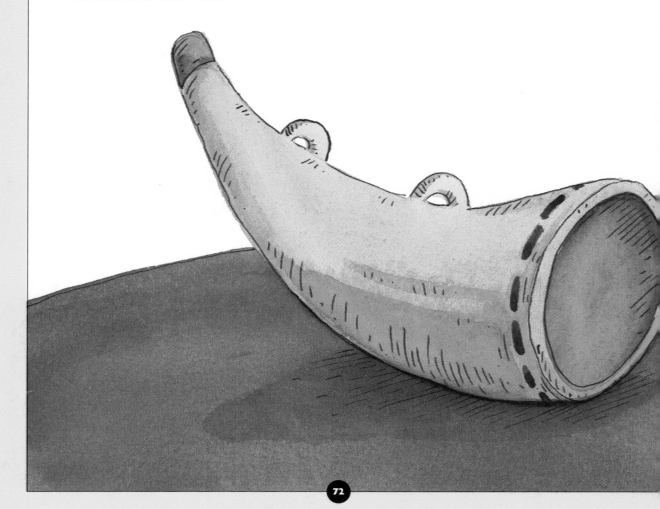

Would you like to have oil poured on your head?

If you lived in Bible times, you might be very glad.

You would be very glad if you were anointed.

What Do Your Parents Do for a Living?

If you lived in Bible times, your dad might work in a vineyard.

He might help in a grain field.

He might squish grape juice through his toes at a wine press.

He might make clay pots with a potter's wheel.

Moms worked, too.

But they worked in the fields to help Dad.

Or they took care of the children.

If your Dad was blind or very sick, he had to beg.

If he could not walk or work, he had to beg.

He had no other way to get money.

These men are slaves. Their children will be slaves, too.

That's the way it was.

One man owed some money. He could not pay it.

The other man was angry.

He made the first man become his slave.

Another man was captured in a battle.

So he became a slave.

Slaves could be bought from a slave trader.

Slaves did chores in a house.

They took care of people.

They worked in the fields.

They carried heavy things for their masters.

They did all kinds of work.

Tell God thank you that you are not a slave!

Saws, Drills, and Hammers

Do you like to go to the hardware store with

Dad or Mom? Most of us do.

What do we see there?

We see hammers. We see electric drills and sanders.

We see saws. Most tools are electric.

Bible-time people did not have electricity.

So there were no electric tools.

So what did carpenters use?

Their tools were different from those today.

Here is a Bible-time saw.

Have you watched anyone drill with an electric drill?

A Bible-time carpenter had a drill.

It was called a bow drill.

This is the way he used it.

Bible-time hammers were made of wood.

What did carpenters make in Bible times?

People needed wagons. They needed wagon wheels.

Of course everyone needed some chairs or stools.

Tables and chests were needed too.

All these things were made from wood.

Even farmers' plows were made of wood.

So everyone needed a carpenter.

Fishing with Peter on the Sea of Galilee

Would you like to go fishing with Peter and his friends?

Peter and his friends need hundreds of fish.

They catch the fish, and sell them.

That's how they make their living.

You won't need fishing hooks.

Catching fish with hooks is too slow.

You need big nets. They are called dragnets.

We must check the nets carefully.

Are there any holes? We must fix them.

Fish could get through those holes.

The boats look like this.

Are you ready? Let's go.

Let's help Peter and his friends push

their boats from the shore.

We launch out now on the Sea of Galilee.

Sometimes we must row these boats.

Sometimes we put up the sails.

The wind will blow the boats across the water.

We must help Peter fasten one end of the big net to his boat.

A friend fastens the other end of the net to his boat.

Let's drop the anchor while we do this.

The anchor is made of stone. It looks like this.

This is how the two boats will pull the dragnet.

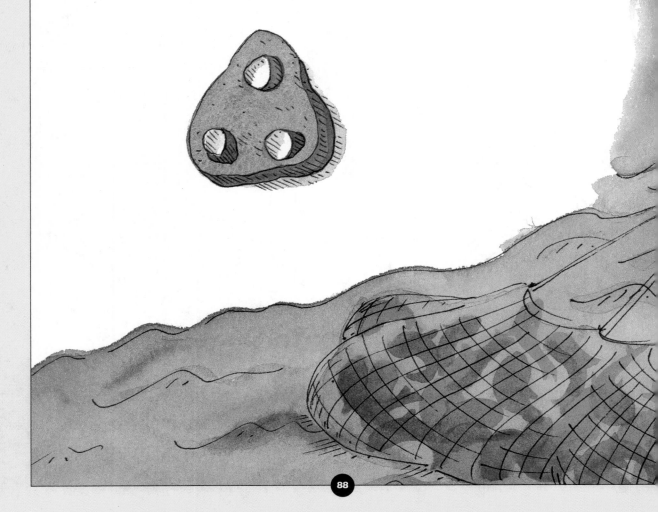

The fish will be trapped in the big net.

Look! We will get many fish today.

Are you ready? We will help pull the nets up.

Do you see all of the fish?

Sometimes Peter and his friends do not fish with their boats.

They stand in the water near the shore.

They use a net like this.

It is called a casting net.

They throw it out.

Then they pull it in.

The net pulls the fish toward them.

What did the fish in the Sea of Galilee look like?

Here are some.

Sometimes Peter and his friends go fishing at night.

One time they worked all night long.

But they did not catch anything.

Then Jesus helped them catch many, many fish.

They were glad Jesus helped them.

Remember to tell God thank you when He helps you.

A Day in the Grain Fields with Ruth

Ruth is gleaning. That's why people call her a gleaner.

She is picking up stalks of grain.

She will grind this grain to make flour.

She will make bread with the flour.

Ruth and Naomi will have bread to eat.

Ruth will work all day in this grain field.

She will work as long as the reapers are harvesting the grain.

Here are some things Ruth will see in the grain fields today.

Reapers cut stalks of grain with sickles.

The sickles look like this.

Other workers tie the stalks together.

They use straw for their string.

These bundles of stalks are called sheaves.

They must lie here to dry.

Do you see what these workers are doing?

They are putting the dry sheaves onto donkeys or camels.

They did not have tractors or other farm machines in Bible times.

Now the workers take the sheaves to the threshing floor.

They carry them with donkeys or camels.

The threshing floor is a big flat place.

It is on a high hill. They need the wind blowing up here.

The workers throw the sheaves onto this flat ground.

Oxen pull a heavy sledge over the sheaves.

This crushes the heads of grain.

It crushes the straw, too.

The wheat or barley grains fall out on the ground.

They are still mixed with the crushed straw.

A worker picks up some of the crushed straw and grain.

He has a big wooden fork.

He throws the straw and grain into the air.

Look at the wind blow the chaff away.

The grains fall down to the threshing floor.

The worker keeps doing this until most of the chaff is gone.

This is called winnowing.

Women are now sifting the grain.

This takes out everything but the grain.

Later the grain will be ground into flour.

People will make bread from this flour.

Bread is the most important food to these people.

The next time you have bread, remember Ruth.

Think how hard Ruth and her friends worked for their bread.

Give thanks to God for your bread today, and for

all the other wonderful food He provides.

Grape Juice Squishing between My Toes

Do you like grape juice?

Would you like to squish it between your toes?

People in Bible times did!

In Bible times, many people had vineyards.

That's where they grew grapes.

When the grapes were ripe, people picked them.

They carried them in baskets.

They brought them to a big stone vat.

This was called a winepress.

Do you see what is happening?

These men squeeze the juice from the grapes.

They do it by stomping on the grapes with their bare feet.

The grape juice squishes between their toes.

It runs out in the smaller stone vat.

People dip the juice from this vat.

They put it in big jars or animal skin bottles.

Would you like to squish this stuff between your toes?

Helping David Take Care of Sheep

Would you like to visit David today?

Would you like to help him take care of his sheep?

Let's go! There is David out in the fields.

He must have a hundred sheep.

The sheep cannot find their own food.

We must lead them to a place with good grass to eat.

They cannot find their own water.

We must lead them to water, too.

Look! One of the little lambs is hurt.

We must carry it until it can walk again.

It's night now.

We will put the sheep into a sheepfold.

This has a fence around it. It will keep out wild animals.

We must sleep at the doorway with David.

No wild animal must get past us.

It's time to sleep.

But we must always be listening.

Nothing can hurt our sheep.

When it's morning, we will help David count his sheep.

If one is missing, we must find it.

Look! Here comes a lion.

He wants to eat one of our sheep.

Get your sling. Get your spear.

Let's be ready to fight the lion.

We cannot let the lion hurt one little lamb.

So be careful, lion.

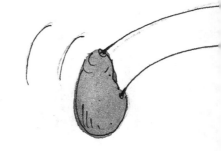

How Can I Write a Letter?

In Bible times, there was no paper like the paper in this book.

Some people in Abraham's time wrote on clay tablets, like this.

People also wrote on animal skins.

Sometimes these skins were rolled into scrolls.

They looked like this.

People also wrote on papyrus.

They made papyrus by hammering plant stems together, like this.

Scrolls were made of papyrus, too.

In Jesus' time people had wooden tablets like this.

A tablet was covered with wax.

People scratched writing into the wax.

They could "erase" their writing by making the wax smooth.

The pens in this picture were made from reeds.

The reeds were stems of plants.

Yes, they had ink, too.

Do you see the ink pot?

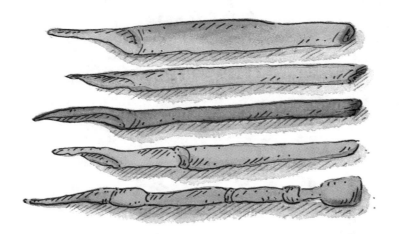

Are you glad for paper?

How would you like to do all your writing on

animals skins or clay?

How would you like to write on papyrus?

Thank You, God, for paper.

It helps me have wonderful books like this.

It helps me have lots of fun writing.

Bible-Time Malls Were Not Like Ours!

Do you like to visit a mall? What do you find there?

You can buy clothing. You can buy food.

You can buy almost anything you want.

In Bible times, people shopped at a marketplace like this.

The mall you visit is open almost every day.

But in Bible times people came to the market only

on certain days.

Farmers and country people brought things to sell.

They brought fruits and vegetables.

They brought other foods they raised.

And some brought sheep or goats to sell.

Merchants set up booths.

They sold things they had bought far away.

These merchants often brought their things on camels.

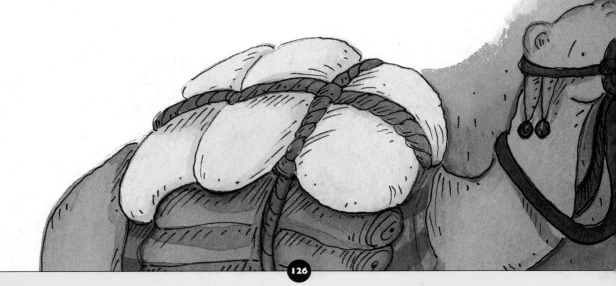

Each thing at the mall you visit has a tag.

It tells you how much this costs.

But Bible-time people did not put tags on their things.

People shouted and argued about the price.

At last the person selling said yes.

Let's Take a Trip

When you and your family take a long trip,

you get into the family car. You drive on beautiful roads.

On the way you stop at filling stations.

You buy gas for your car.

Perhaps you get some ice cream at the filling station.

Do you need a rest room? The filling station has that.

Where will you stay at night?

There are many hotels and motels to choose from.

What about dinner? There are many restaurants.

Which one would you like?

So let's take a trip.

But you are in Bible times now.

You can't take the family car. They didn't have cars.

You can't drive on beautiful roads.

They had roads in Jesus' time, but they were not like ours.

You can't go on a bus or train or airplane either.

There were no such things.

Could you ride on a motorbike?

No, sorry. And there were no trucks or vans or

streetcars or anything like that.

You probably would walk.

Most people walked when they went places.

They walked many, many miles.

If your family had more money, you might have a donkey.

One of you could ride the donkey.

Or the donkey might carry your things.

Your family might not go alone.

There are too many robbers along the way.

They could hurt you.

People traveled together.

When they did, they were called caravans.

Look at that man.

He has enough money to get a camel.

He can travel faster and farther than he could on a donkey.

Perhaps you need to take lots of things along.

You may have a cart or wagon.

Your whole family may get into the cart or wagon.

It's slow going.

Two oxen will probably pull the cart or wagon.

They don't win any races.

But they get there. So do you.

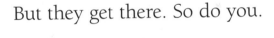

It's time to stop for the night.

Bible-time people did not have motels like ours.

They had inns.

Inns looked like this.

Bible-time inns did not have signs.

You had to ask other people where to find them.

The inn had a place for your donkey or camel to get water.

But there were no restaurants.

People brought their own food.

Bible-time inns did not have beds.

People brought their own sleeping pads.

They did not have soft pillows.

People did not use pillows much.

The inn was not as nice as a motel today.

But it was a safe place to stay.

Thank You, Lord, for my safe home!

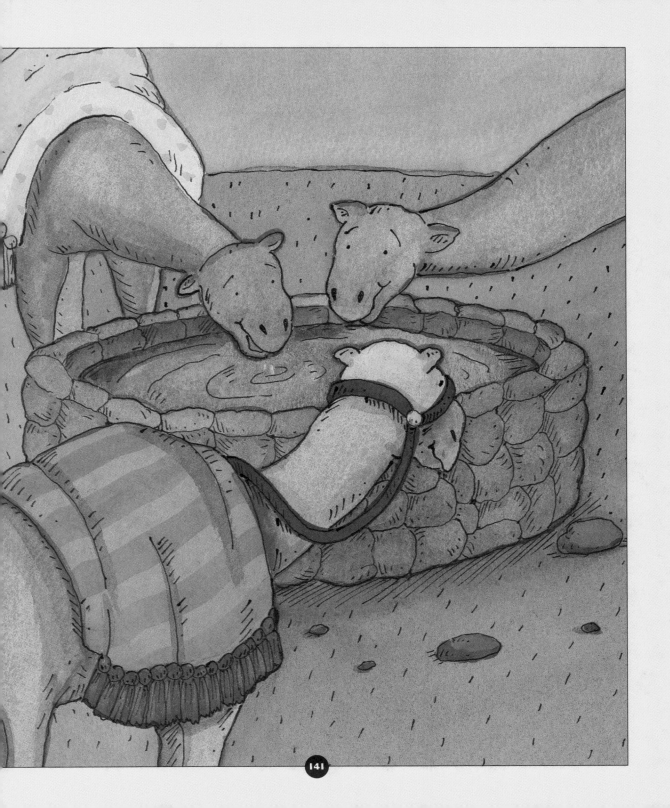

Soldiers and Their Weapons

Think of the things soldiers fight with today.

Bible-time soldiers did not have most of these weapons.

Bible-time soldiers did not have machine guns.

They did not have any guns or bullets.

They did not have bombs or mines.

Instead, they used swords, spears, bows, and arrows.

Do you remember the sling David used?

He killed Goliath with it.

Slings were not just toys for shepherd boys.

They were weapons used by soldiers.

Bible-time people did not have airplanes.

They did not have submarines.

There were no tanks like ours.

But they did have chariots.

A chariot was a powerful weapon in Bible times.

It was something like a tank.

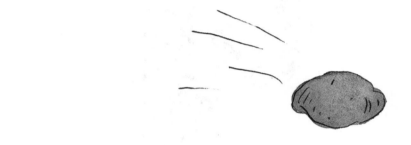

Now look at this other weapon.

It was a mean one.

It was called a battering ram.

How would you like one of these at your door tonight?

Thank You, Lord, for each day of peace.

Thank You that I can sleep quietly tonight in my home.

I'm glad I don't have a battering ram knocking on my door.

The Bullet-proof Vest of Bible Times

There were no bullets in Bible times.

That's because there were no guns.

But metal armor like this could stop a bullet.

It kept arrows and spears from getting through.

It kept its owners from getting killed.

How would you like to wear a big metal shirt like this?

You wouldn't want to play ball in it.

But it would be great if someone shot an arrow at you!

Will You Please Get Off My Neck?

That king isn't very nice, is he?

He's stepping on that other man's neck. Ouch!

The king on the ground is King Zedekiah.

He was King of Judah.

The king stepping on him is an Assyrian king.

He just captured Zedekiah.

That's why he is stepping on Zedekiah's neck.

It was a way of saying, "I won!"

Aren't you glad we don't do that today?

Going to Prison

You wouldn't want to be put into prison, would you?

It is not easy. But it was much harder in Bible times.

Paul was put into prison many times.

He told people about Jesus.

Some people did not like that.

Sometimes they put him in prison.

People in prison often had to

wear chains, like this.

Sometimes a prisoner was chained to a guard.

Paul had a guard like that in Rome.

Or sometimes they were put into stocks like this.

Paul and Silas were in stocks at the prison at Philippi.

Today we have buildings called prisons.

In Bible times there were not many prisons.

Sometimes prisoners were kept in rooms dug out

under the ground.

Jeremiah was put into a cistern, like this.

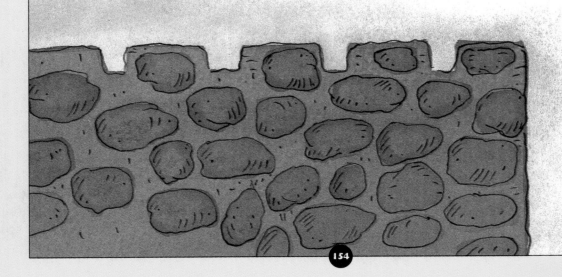

Sometimes people were punished before they

were put into prison.

They might be whipped like this.

This was called scourging.

Jesus was scourged by Roman soldiers.

Sometimes people were stoned.

They never went to prison after stoning.

Stoning killed them.

Some people who could not pay debts were put into prison.

Prisons were hard places in Bible times.

Aren't you glad this is only a visit?

Thank You, Lord, that you make me free!